D0843124

Sports Illustrated KIDS
FOOTBALL Jokes

by Blake Hoena

illustrated by Daryll Colins

STONE ARCH BOOKS
a capstone imprint

Sports Illustrated Kids All-Star Jokes
is published by Stone Arch Books, a Capstone imprint
1710 Roe Crest Drive
North Mankato, Minnesota 56003
www.mycapstone.com

Cataloging-in-Publication data is available
on the Library of Congress website.

ISBN: 978-1-4965-5093-4 (library binding)
ISBN: 978-1-4965-5097-2 (eBook pdf)

Summary: SPORTS ILLUSTRATED KIDS presents an all-star collection of
FOOTBALL jokes, riddles, and memes! With grid-iron one-liners like "Why
did the football coach go to the bank? He wanted his quarter back!" these
colorful, illustrated joke books will have FOOTBALL fans rolling in the
stadium aisles.

Designer: Brann Garvey

Photo Credits:
Sports Illustrated: Bill Frakes, 57, David E. Klutho, 36, John Biever, 14, John
W. McDonough, 28, 32, Peter Read Miller, 42, Robert Beck, 24, Simon Bruty, 4

Printed and bound in the United States of America
042018   000022

CONTENTS

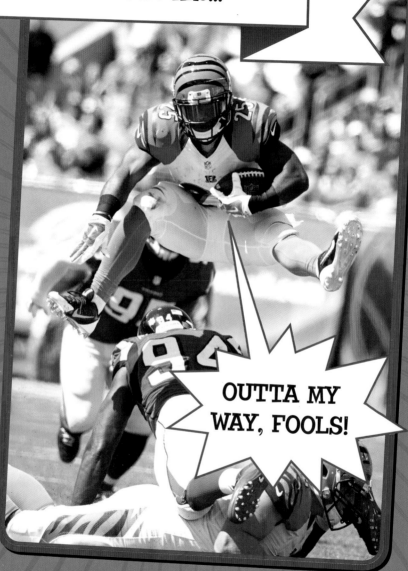

CHAPTER 1

On the Gridiron

What do football players
pour their cereal into?

Super Bowls.

What do football players like
to eat before a big game?

Hut-hut-hutdogs!

What do you get when receivers don't
lift weights on weekdays?

Weak ends.

When is a football player
like a judge?

When he sits on
the bench!

What's the difference between
a quarterback and a baby?

One takes the snap while the
other takes a nap.

Why don't football teams
play doubleheaders?

Because coaches only give
each player one helmet.

How come the football player
didn't score a touchdown?

Because his flight was
stuck in a holding pattern.

Why did the woman shout "hut-hut"
before she went "achoo!"?

Because it was
football sneezin'!

Where do astronauts play football?

On Astroturf!

What type of insects are
bad at football?

Fumble-bees!

What did one raindrop say to the other raindrops falling on the field?

Okay, let's puddle up!

Why did the tiny ghost join the football team?

He heard they needed a little team spirit.

Where do hungry football players play?

In the Supper Bowl.

What kind of ends do you find in libraries?

Book ends.

Why wasn't the receiver
very successful?

Opportunities always
slipped through his fingers.

What position did the pile
of wood play on the
football team?

De-fence!

What do you get when you cross a
football player with a gorilla?

I don't know, but
nobody would try to stop
it from scoring!

Why is an airplane pilot
like a football player?

They both make
touchdowns.

When you finish your math test with time to spare...

CHAPTER 2

Punny Positions

What position does a
tough-looking pig play?

Swinebacker!

Why don't eggs make good
quarterbacks?

They're too quick
to scramble!

Why do coaches like kickers the most?

Because they put their
best foot forward.

Which is the easiest player
to throw to?

The wiiiiiiiiiide receiver!

What kind of player gives refunds?

A quarterback.

What did the football
say to the punter?

"I get a kick out of you!"

Where's the best place to
buy presents for a linebacker?

A tackle shop.

Where do quarterbacks go to retire?

Out to pass-ture.

Which football player wears
the biggest helmet?

The one with the biggest head!

Why was the centipede dropped
from the insect football team?

He took too long
to put on his cleats!

Why aren't there Swiss linemen?

Because they always line up
in the neutral zone.

What is black and white
and red all over?

A referee with
a sunburn!

Why did the town use the football
stadium as its tornado shelter?

Because there had never
been a touchdown there.

Why did you lineman write
T.G.I.F on his cleats?

To remember that
"Toes Go In First!"

What happened when the quarterback
told his receivers a joke?

Just like his passes,
it went over their heads!

What football play should
you be suspicious of?

The quarterback
sneak.

What are the three most
popular sports in Texas?

Pro football, college football,
and high school football!

Why didn't the skeleton want
to play running back?

His heart wasn't in it!

How does a star quarterback
change a light bulb?

He holds it up and lets the
world revolve around him.

Why did the frog want to play
football so badly?

He always felt at home
in the pads.

Why did the referee give the hairstylist a penalty flag?

Because he was always spiking the ball!

Why did the coach tell the quarterback to hit the showers?

Because he stunk!

Walking into class when your homework is finished...

CHAPTER 3

Five Yards for Laughing!

What do football players
drink at parties?

Penal-tea.

Where do football players dance?

At foot-balls!

How do you stop squirrels
playing football?

Hide their ball —
it drives them nuts!

What happened to the
retired quarterback?

He just passed away.

Why did the football player sell
one of his five homes?

He didn't want a
five-yard penalty.

Why did the running back
stop in the middle of a play to
sing the national anthem?

Because there was a
flag on the play.

Why are dogs horrible
football players?

They're always ruffing
the passer!

Why did the chicken cross the football field?

The referee called a foul!

When you forget that
it's picture day...

CHAPTER 4

Fanatic Fans

Who are the happiest people
at a football game?

The cheerleaders!

How do chickens cheer
for their team?

By egging them on.

What is a football cheerleader's
favorite color?

Yeller!

Why was the football stadium
packed with cheering pigs?

They all had skin
in the game.

What is a football cheerleader's
favorite food?

Cheerios!

What is a cheerleader's
favorite drink?

Root beer!

How do football players read
all their fan mail?

They breeze through
most of it.

Any of you
guys know the rules?

CHAPTER 5

Rowdy Refs

What's black and white
and never right?

A football referee!

Why did the ref call a
penalty on the dog?

For ruffing the passer.

What happened when the coach
asked for onions instead of pickles
on his hamburger?

The waitress penalized him
for an illegal substitution.

Why didn't the football
player like going trick-or-treating?

He kept getting penalized
for his facemask.

How can you tell that football
referees are patriotic?

They're always
carrying a flag.

What animal would make the
best football referee?

A canary — because it already
knows how to whistle.

Why are referees the
worst kind of neighbors?

They're always taking
away yards!

CHAPTER 6

Kooky Coaches

Why did the coach start filling the
stadium up with water?

She wanted a sub to
enter the game.

Why did the coach retire
due to illness?

The fans were sick of him!

Why did the football coach
decide to open a bakery?

He knew a lot
about turnovers!

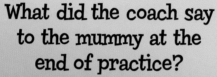

What did the coach say
to the mummy at the
end of practice?

Let's wrap this up!

Why didn't the nose make the basketball team?

The coach never picked it.

PLAYER: Coach, the doctor said
I can't play football.

COACH: You didn't need a doctor
to figure that out!

Why did the clock leave
the football game?

The coach called
time out!

Why did the coach send his toddler
onto the football field?

Because his team
needed someone who
could block!

Why did the coach trade his
running back for a dollar bill?

He knew he could get four
quarters out of a dollar.

What did the quarterback
say when the coach asked if he
wanted to hear a joke?

No, thanks — I'll pass.

Why did the coach cut the
candy bar from his team?

Because it was
a Butterfinger.

Why didn't the coach
draft the puppy?

It was a boxer!

What was the difference
between the coach's nickel defense
and dime defense?

About five cents.

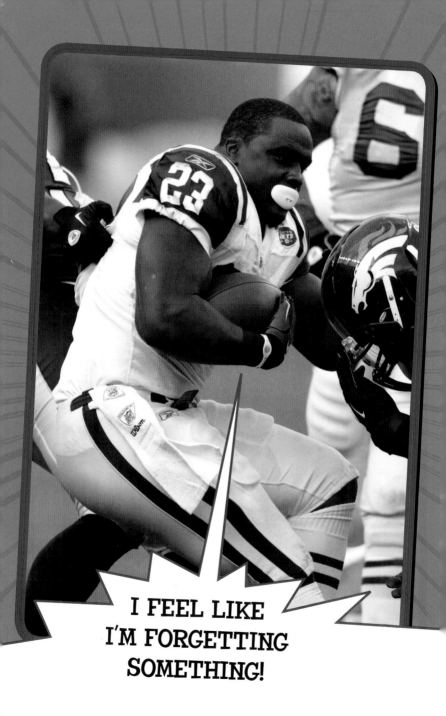

I FEEL LIKE I'M FORGETTING SOMETHING!

CHAPTER 7
All-Laugh Team

What team did the rhino
want to play for?

The San Diego Chargers!

Which football team cooks
the best food?

The Kansas City Chefs.

How do you sack the
Dolphins' quarterback?

With fishing tackle!

How much do Tampa Bay
players get paid?

A buck-an-ear.

Why is MetLife Stadium the
coolest place to be?

Because of all the
Giant fans.

Why don't the Steelers like
playing at Heinz field?

Because they're always
playing ketchup.

Why couldn't the Seahawks'
quarterback use the phone?

He couldn't find
the receiver.

How many Detroit Lions
does it take to win
a Super Bowl?

Nobody knows!

Why doesn't anyone trust
Pittsburgh's football team?

Because they're Steelers!

What do you call a Chicago
player with no teeth?

A gummy bear!

Why is Jacksonville's team
called the Jaguars and not
the Cheetahs?

Because no one would
want to play them if they
were Cheethas!

Why couldn't the Bears win
all winter long?

They were supposed to
be hibernating!

Why do the Cowboys ride
horses to the game?

Because they're too
heavy to carry!

Why do the New England Patriots
always end up with the most flags?

They have to live up
to their name.

What should you put in the
end zone to keep the
Ravens away?

A scorecrow!

What football player smells
the nicest?

The scenter (center).

Why are the New York Jets
like lawmakers?

They both push
around Bills.

Why do New Orleans fans call
their Saints a "Dream Team"?

Because they can only dream
of another championship!

Why don't the Minnesota Vikings
have any women on their team?

They all play for
the ViQUEENS!

How many Green Bay running backs
does it take to change a light bulb?

Two — one to screw
it in and the other to
recover the fumble.

Why did the Browns cut
their quarterback?

Because he was
feeling blue.

What team never has any money
but is always willing to pay?

The Chargers.

Why can't the Browns'
running back get into his
own driveway?

Someone painted it took
look like an end zone!

Where do football teams buy
their uniforms?

New Jersey!

Why are the Miami Hurricanes
always dropping balls?

Because Hurricanes only
have one eye.

Why do the Oregon Ducks practice
more than any team?

Because they're always up
at the quack of dawn.

Why don't Florida Gators
like fast food?

Because they
can't catch it!

Why wasn't the Oklahoma
football team worried about
their losing streak?

They knew they'd win
Sooners or later.

Why doesn't Iowa have
a professional football team?

Because then Minnesota
would want one too.

What do both teams lose in
a football game?

Their breath!

What do you call a basement
filled with Patriot fans?

A whine cellar.

Which Houston Texans
player gives refunds?

A quarterback.

How did the 49ers beat
the Cardinals?

They scored more
points than them!

What happened when the Rams
returned their draft pick?

They only got halfback.

NO MORE JOKES?!?!

How to Tell Jokes

1. KNOW the joke.

Make sure you remember the whole joke before you tell it. This sounds like a no-brainer, but most of us have known someone who says, "Oh, this is so funny . . ." Then, when they tell the joke, they can't remember the end. And that's the whole point of a joke — its punch line.

2. SPEAK CLEARLY.

Don't mumble; don't speak too fast or too slow. Just speak like you normally do. You don't have to use a different voice or accent or sound like someone else. (UNLESS that's part of the joke!)

3. LOOK at your audience.

Good eye contact with your listeners will grab their attention.

4. DON'T WORRY about gestures or how to stand or sit when you tell your joke. Remember, telling a joke is basically talking.

5. DON'T LAUGH at your own joke.

Yeah, yeah, I know some comedians break up while they're acting in a sketch or telling a story, but the best rule to follow is not to laugh. If you start to laugh, you might lose the rhythm of your joke or keep yourself from telling the joke clearly. Let your audience laugh. That's their job. Your job is to be the funny one.

6. THE PUNCH LINE is the most important part of the joke.

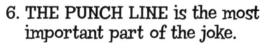

It's the climax, the payoff, the main event. A good joke can sound even better if you pause for just a second or two before you deliver the punch line. That tiny pause will make your audience mentally sit up and hold their breath, eager to hear what's coming next.

7. The SETUP is the second most important part of a joke.

That's basically everything you say before you get to the punch line. And that's why you need to be as clear as you can (see 2 above) so that when you finally reach the punch line, it makes sense!

8. YOU CAN GET FUNNIER.

It's easy. Watch other comedians. Listen to other people tell a joke or story. Check out a good comedy show or film. You can pick up some skills simply by seeing how others get their comedy across. You will absorb it! And soon it will come naturally.

9. Last, but not least, telling a joke is all about TIMING.

That means not only getting the biggest impact for your joke, waiting for the right time, giving that extra pause before the punch line — but it also means knowing when NOT to tell a joke. When you're among friends, you can tell when they'd like to hear something funny. But in an unfamiliar setting, get a "sense of the room" first. Are people having a good time? Or is it a more serious event? A joke has the most funny power when it's told in the right setting.

BLAKE HOENA

Blake Hoena grew up in central Wisconsin. In his youth, he wrote stories about robots conquering the moon and trolls lumbering around the woods behind his parents' house. He now lives in St. Paul, Minnesota, with his wife, two kids, a dog, and a couple of cats. Blake continues to make up stories about things like space aliens and superheroes, and he has written more than 70 chapter books, graphic novels, and joke books for children.

DARYLL COLLINS

Daryll Collins is a professional illustrator in the areas of magazine & newspaper illustration, children's books, character design & development, advertising, comic strips, greeting cards, games, and more! His clients range from Sports Illustrated Kids and Boys' Life magazine to McDonald's and the US Postal Service. He currently lives in Kentucky.

Joke Dictionary!

bit (BIT)—a section of a comedy routine

comedian (kuh-MEE-dee-uhn)—an entertainer who makes people laugh

headliner (HED-lye-ner)—the last comedian to perform in a show

improvisation (im-PRAH-vuh-ZAY-shuhn)—a performance that hasn't been planned; "improv" for short

lineup (LINE-uhp)—a list of people who are going to perform in a show

one-liner (WUHN-lye-ner)—a short joke or funny remark

open mike (OH-puhn MIKE)—an event at which anyone can use the microphone to perform for the audience

punch line (PUHNCH line)—the words at the end of a joke that make it funny or surprising

shtick (SHTIK)—a repetitive, comic performance or routine

segue (SEG-way)—a sentence or phrase that leads from one joke or routine to another

stand-up (STAND-uhp)—a stand-up comedian performs while standing alone on stage

timing (TIME-ing)—the use of rhythm and tempo to make the joke funnier

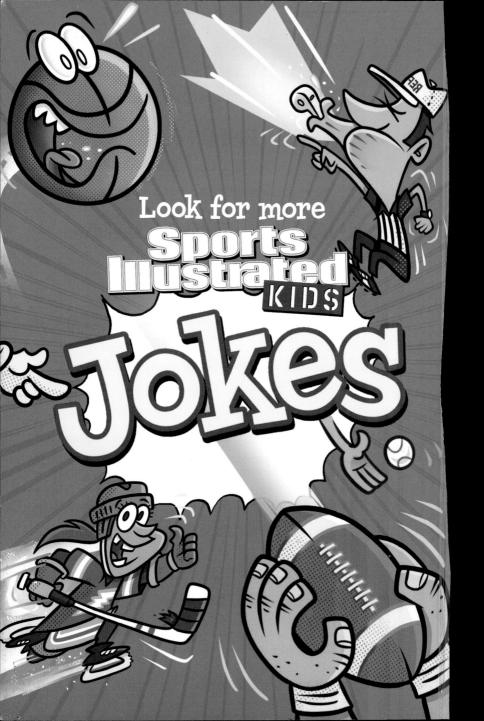

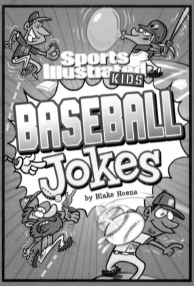

Sports Illustrated KIDS

BASEBALL Jokes

by Blake Hoena

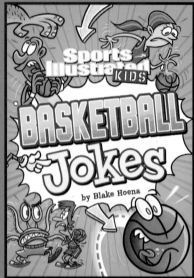

Sports Illustrated KIDS

BASKETBALL Jokes

by Blake Hoena

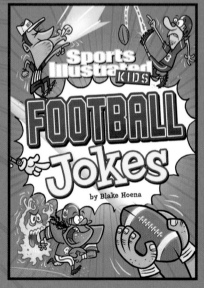

Sports Illustrated KIDS

FOOTBALL Jokes

by Blake Hoena

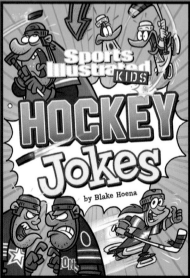

Sports Illustrated KIDS

HOCKEY Jokes

by Blake Hoena

FACTHOUND

Use FactHound to find Internet sites related to this book.

Visit www.facthound.com

Just type in 9781496550934 and go.

 Check out projects, games and lots more at
www.capstonekids.com